# INTERNET ANIMAL STARS

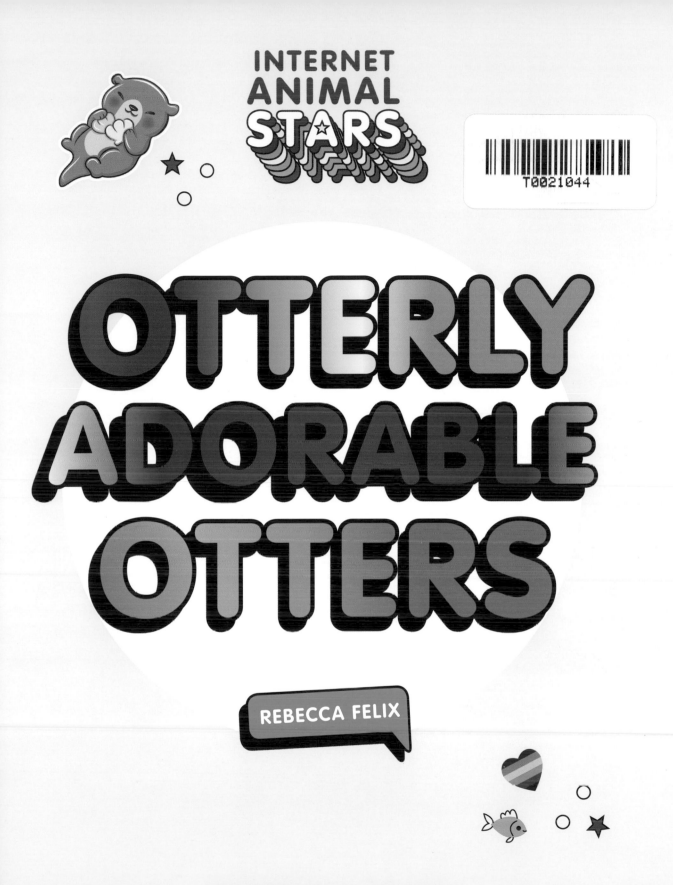

# OTTERLY ADORABLE OTTERS

REBECCA FELIX

Lerner Publications ◆ Minneapolis

Lerner Publications Company
An imprint of Lerner Publishing Group, Inc.
241 First Avenue North
Minneapolis, MN 55401 USA

For reading levels and more information, look up this title at www.lernerbooks.com.
Main body text set in Caecilia Com
Typeface provided by Monotype

Library of Congress Cataloging-in-Publication Data

Names: Felix, Rebecca, 1984– author.
Title: Otterly adorable otters / Rebecca Felix.
Description: Minneapolis : Lerner Publications, [2021] | Series: Internet animal stars | Includes bibliographical references and index. | Audience: Ages 6–10 | Audience: Grades 2–3 | Summary: "Adorable otters are everywhere: in rivers, in oceans, and on the internet! A playful design inspired by social media will draw in young readers, while lively factual text explains their life cycle and habitat"— Provided by publisher.
Identifiers: LCCN 2019058468 (print) | LCCN 2019058469 (ebook) | ISBN 9781541597150 (library binding) | ISBN 9781728402901 (paperback) | ISBN 9781728400389 (ebook)
Subjects: LCSH: Otters—Juvenile literature.
Classification: LCC QL737.C25 F45 2021  (print) | LCC QL737.C25  (ebook) | DDC 599.769—dc23

LC record available at https://lccn.loc.gov/2019058468
LC ebook record available at https://lccn.loc.gov/2019058469

Manufactured in the United States of America
1 – CG – 7/15/20

PAGE
PLUS
+

Scan QR codes throughout the book
for videos of cute animals!

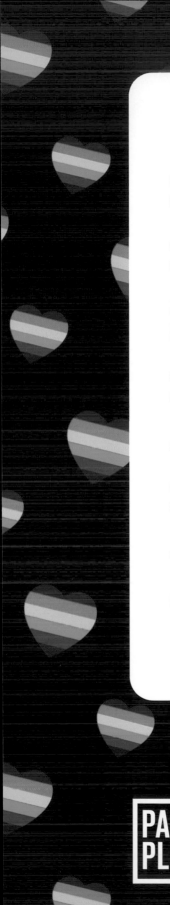

# OTTERLY ADORABLE OTTERS

What do you know about otters? These **aquatic** animals are in the weasel family. There are several otter species. Humans love otters! The internet is swimming with comical otter **content**. Dive into facts about these creatures. Then find out how otters became internet famous!

## #WeaselSquad

Badgers, ferrets, and wolverines are also part of the weasel family.

I'm otter this world!

# Chapter 1

# OTTER EVOLUTION

## ★ Fluffy Pups ★

Baby otters are called pups. They are born underwater or in dens on land. Pups weigh up to 5 pounds (2 kg).

Pups **nurse** from birth. After a few weeks, they also eat solid foods.

Newborn pups have thick, fluffy fur. It traps air. This air makes it impossible to dive! Newborn pups just float.

Scan this QR code to see a baby sea otter with its mother!

# Growing Up Otter

At three months, an otter's adult fur comes in.

There are thirteen otter species. Two are **marine**. Otter species **vary** in size. Some are just 7 pounds (3 kg). Others grow to 99 pounds (45 kg)!

Otter fur is shades of brown.

#FurFact
Sea otter fur is so thick that water can't pass through it. An otter's skin never gets wet!

# ★ Elder ★ Otters

River otters have few water **predators**. On land, wolves and bears are threats. Wild river otters live about nine years.

Wild sea otters live longer. Females can live up to twenty years.

Sharks and killer whales prey on sea otters.

# Chapter 2

# IN OTTER WORLDS

River otters live in Canada, the United States, Europe, Asia, and North Africa. They spend time on land and in water.

River otters make dens along the water. The animals eat fish, crabs, frogs, birds, and turtles. Some eat plants and small mammals like rabbits.

Otterly lost in thought!

#SwimmerBod

Otters have long tails that propel them through water.

Sea otters live off the coasts of California, Alaska, and Russia.

Sea otters eat sea urchins, clams, mussels, crabs, and snails. They use tools for eating. Sea otters float on their backs and use rocks to bash open animal shells.

Sea otters spend most of their lives in water!

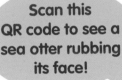

Scan this QR code to see a sea otter rubbing its face!

#PitPockets

Sea otters store rocks in armpit skin folds. These folds are like pockets!

Sea otters are social. They live in groups. Females and pups form one group. Males form another.

River otters usually live alone or in pairs.

Scan this QR code to see a river otter slip and slide!

Both river and sea otters are **curious** and playful. Happy otters charm the online world.

**So do silly otters, smart otters, and sleepy otters!**

# Chapter 3

# OTTERS IN POP CULTURE

Otters are internet stars! But how and why did these water weasels gain online fame?

A 2007 video helped. That year, the Vancouver **Aquarium** posted a video of two sleeping otters holding hands. It went **viral**. More otter content followed.

#Starstruck

Researchers say otters are **beloved** because people think they are cute!

People also think of otters as **energetic** and fun-loving. Fictional otters in books and films are usually presented this way.

These ideas about otters have led some to become social media celebrities.

#OtterSquad

# ★ Otter Idols ★

Otters become internet famous for many reasons. Some star in a single meme. Others are regularly featured on zoo or aquarium social media accounts, websites, and more!

# Superstar! ABBY

Abby lived at the Monterey Bay Aquarium in 2018. That year, the aquarium posted a photo of Abby joking that she was overweight. The post went viral from people defending the chunky otter. Abby became an online star.

MEME BREAK!

ME WHEN MOM SAYS IT'S TIME TO GET OUT OF THE POOL

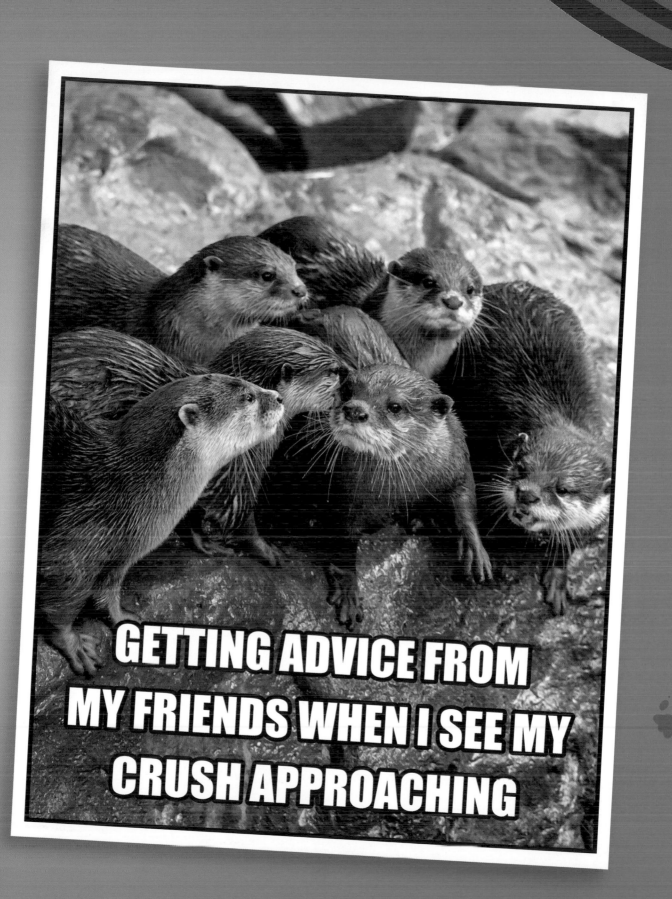

GETTING ADVICE FROM MY FRIENDS WHEN I SEE MY CRUSH APPROACHING

WAITING FOR THE TEACHER TO EXCUSE THE CLASS FOR RECESS

LAUGHING AT MY OWN DUMB JOKES LIKE

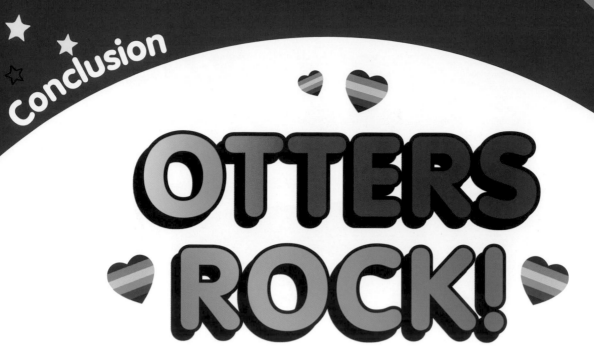

# OTTERS ROCK!

Otters have been online stars for years! This has led to trends offline too.

One is negative. Some people keep otters as pets. Scientists say this is unhealthy. Otters are meant to live in the wild.

On World Otter Day, people celebrate the animals and raise awareness about otter **conservation**.

Otter popularity has led people to protect them.

#OtterStar

**aquarium:** a building in which fish and other underwater animals or plants are exhibited

**aquatic:** living in or found near water

**beloved:** loved very much

**conservation:** the protection of something

**content:** ideas, facts, and images available online

**curious:** wanting to know more about something

**energetic:** having a lot of energy

**marine:** relating to the sea

**nurse:** to drink milk from a mother's body

**predator:** an animal that eats other animals to survive

**vary:** to be different

**viral:** spreading quickly to many people over the internet